Road Trip

Monkey and his friend Giraffe are setting out on their vacation.
They love to travel the open road.

Illustrated by Jannie Ho

Community Garden

On Saturday mornings everybody gathers to work in the neighborhood garden.

Illustrated by Sally Springer

Sprinkler Run

These friends like to play in the sprinkler to cool off on a hot day.

Illustrated by Timothy Davis

Harriet's Hats

Harriet tries on every hat she owns before she decides which one to wear.

Illustrated by Mary Sullivan

Amusement Park

Everyone has a favorite ride at the amusement park.
Which ride do you like best?

Illustrated by David Helton

Clip and Comb

Ruff always sits quietly for his haircut, especially when Dina and Billy give him treats and praise.

Illustrated by Paula Pertile

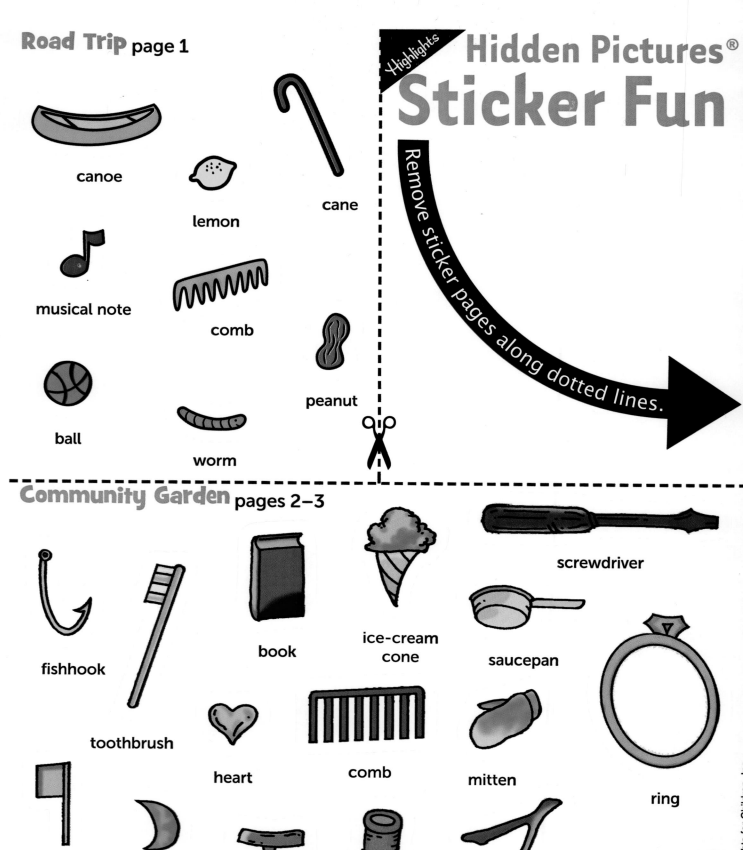

Road Trip page 1

Hidden Pictures®
Sticker Fun

Highlights

Remove sticker pages along dotted lines.

canoe

lemon

cane

musical note

comb

peanut

ball

worm

Community Garden pages 2–3

fishhook

toothbrush

book

ice-cream cone

screwdriver

saucepan

ring

heart

comb

mitten

flag

crescent moon

tack

spool of thread

wishbone

pencil

4244A-07 © Highlights for Children, Inc.

Clip and Comb page 8

candy cane

ladle

loaf of bread

leaf

slice of pizza

ladder

tube of toothpaste

high-heeled shoe

Under Construction page 9

slice of bread

ice-cream cone

fish

top hat

closed book

golf club

toothbrush

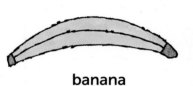

banana

Bill's Bakery page 10

pen

comb

ice-cream cone

drinking straw

dragonfly

candle

golf club

leaf

Mini Golf page 11

sock

pencil

slice of pie

umbrella

horseshoe

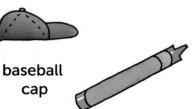

baseball cap

crayon

tent

4244R-07 © Highlights for Children, Inc.

Class Picture pages 12–13

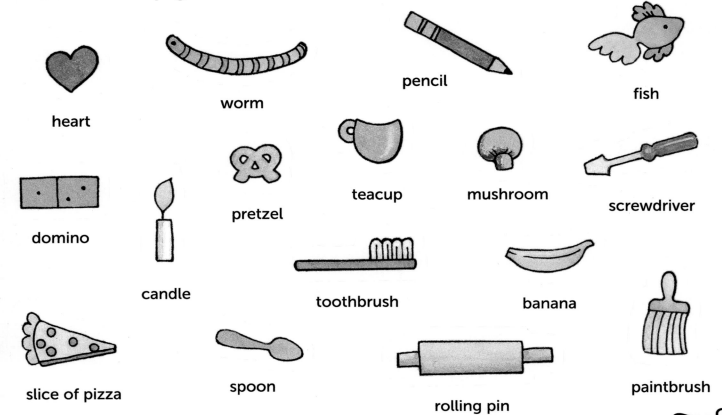

heart

worm

pencil

fish

domino

candle

pretzel

teacup

mushroom

screwdriver

toothbrush

banana

slice of pizza

spoon

rolling pin

paintbrush

Soccer Practice page 14

teacup

horseshoe

ice-cream bar

spoon

bird

baseball

pencil

banana

Shopping List page 15

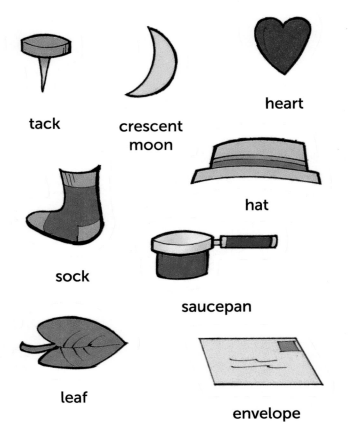

tack

crescent moon

heart

hat

sock

saucepan

leaf

envelope

4244B-07

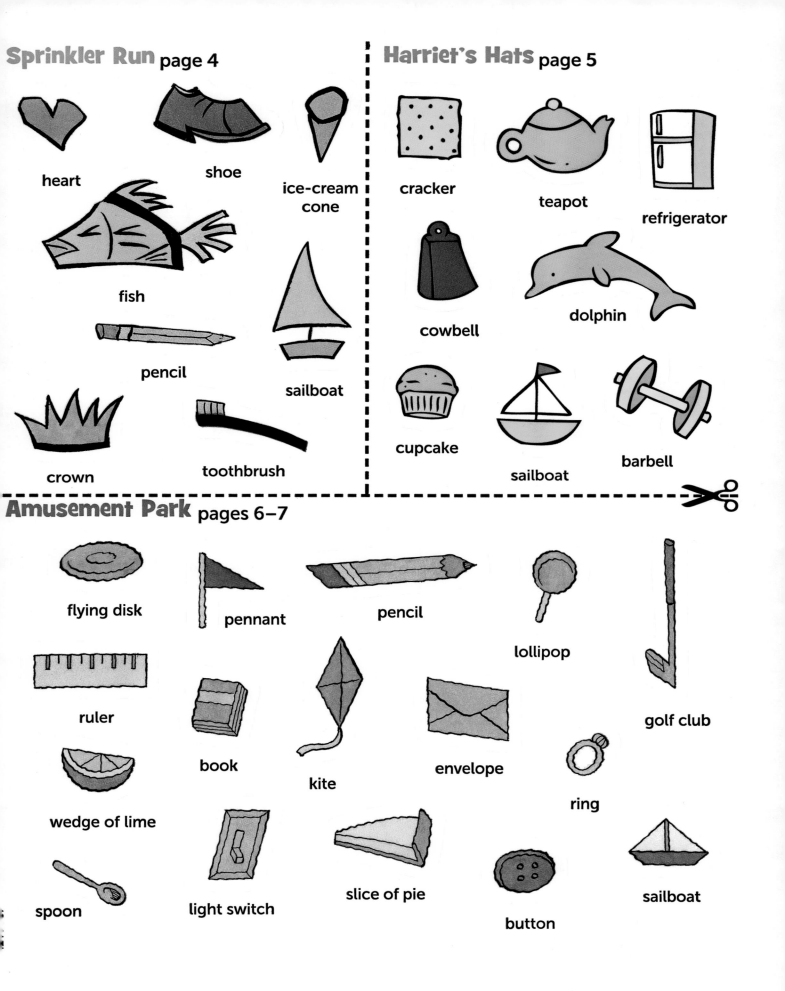

Sprinkler Run page 4

heart

shoe

ice-cream cone

fish

pencil

sailboat

crown

toothbrush

Harriet's Hats page 5

cracker

teapot

refrigerator

cowbell

dolphin

cupcake

sailboat

barbell

Amusement Park pages 6–7

flying disk

pennant

pencil

lollipop

golf club

ruler

book

kite

envelope

ring

wedge of lime

spoon

light switch

slice of pie

button

sailboat

Under Construction

These workers are building a row of houses.
When they are finished, new families will move in.

Illustrated by Viki Woodworth

Bill's Bakery

Jessie and Ben are helping Grandpa buy a cake for Grandma's birthday party. Which one will they choose?

Illustrated by Ron Lieser

10

Mini Golf

Today is Pig's birthday. After he and his friends finish their game, they will have cake and ice cream.

Illustrated by C. S. Forrest

Class Picture

All of Miss Lion's students are wearing their best outfits for picture day at school.

Illustrated by Maggie Swanson

Miss Lion's 1st Grade Class

Soccer Practice

The Dolphins practice every day after school to get ready for their match with the Ravens.

Illustrated by R. Michael Palan

Shopping List

The Turtles fill their grocery cart with their favorite fruits and vegetables.

Illustrated by Rocky Fuller

Answers

Road Trip **page 1**

Community Garden **pages 2–3**

Sprinkler Run **page 4**

Harriet's Hats **page 5**

Amusement Park **pages 6–7**